Marge Piercy is th[...]ng *The Longing of W[...]ne* Arthur C. Clarke [...], *Gone to Soldiers, Woman on [...]ne*, and her most recent, *City of Dark[...]y of Light*. She has also written thirteen collections of poetry including *Circles on the Water* (her selected poems in the States), *The Eight Chambers of the Heart* (selected poems in Britain), *Mars and Her Children, Available Light, My Mother's Body* and most recently, *What Are Big Girls Made Of?* She lives on Cape Cod with her husband, the novelist Ira Wood. Her work has been translated into sixteen languages.

Marge Piercy's *The Art of Blessing the Day: Poems on Jewish Themes* is available from Five Leaves.

Written in Bone

WRITTEN IN BONE

*The Early Poems
of Marge Piercy*

Five Leaves

Written in Bone

Published in 1998 by Five Leaves Publications,
PO Box 81, Nottingham NG5 4ER, Great Britain

Published with financial assistance from

EAST
MIDLANDS
ARTS

East Midlands Arts

Copyright © Middlemarsh Inc.

Design by 4 Sheets
Printed in Great Britain by Antony Rowe

ISBN 0 907123 97 X

PREFACE

I have selected poems from four out of print books, **BREAKING CAMP, LIVING IN THE OPEN, HARD LOVING** and **THE TWELVE-SPOKED WHEEL FLASHING.** The book marches backwards until it gets to poems written when I was sixteen, not only uncollected but previously unpublished. A long time ago and almost another person — but I remember her well.

The fifth section consists of previously uncollected poems written over the last twenty five years. Poems get left out of a book for various reasons — need to cut the manuscript, too many love poems or political poems or nature poems or whatever. Perhaps they slipped through a crack in the computer. Every time I change word processing programs, some poems go astray. I may have believed they were in a collection already. Often I simply mislaid or forgot them. Going through my files and old discs, I found a great pile of these, most of which I cannot date. I chose some that I particularly liked for this volume.

Marge Piercy

CONTENTS

From THE TWELVE-SPOKED WHEEL FLASHING

The meaningful exchange	3
Five thousand miles	4
The summer invasion, and the fall	5
Nothing you can have	8
Archipelago	11
The first salad of March	14
Exodus	15
Ask me for anything else	17
What is permitted	19
A gift of light	21
Short season	25
Ghosts	27
The new novel	29
Women of letters	30

From LIVING IN THE OPEN

The token woman	37
The clearest joy	39
Make me feel it	40
Sage and rue	42
River road, high toss	44
Paradise Hollow	45
Kneeling here, I feel good	46
16 in 53	47
The big one	48
There is no known way to tickle a clam	49
Two higher mammals	50
Beautiful weeper	51
The legacy	52

The consumer	53
A short dark turning	54
For a Brazilian 'Bandit'	56
The box	58
January thaw	59
Phases of the sun	61
Lies	62
For Inez Garcia	65

From **HARD LOVING**

Easy	71
Joy as a point	72
The fisherman	73
Your eyes are hard, and other surprises	74
I still feel you	75
Missing person	76
Song of the nudge	77
This is a poem for you	78
Reopening	79
Rain falls on Ioannina	80
To grow on	81
The morning half-life blues	82

From **BREAKING CAMP**

A kid on her way	87
How you stare	88
Dismissal	89
Lapsed	90
Lipsky on Ninth Avenue	92
The miracle	93
Clinic hallway	94
Sunday evening	95

The simplification	96
August	97
August submerging	98
Night of the bear and polar light	99
Exactly how I pursue you	100
Running toward R	101

EARLY, EARLY POEMS

Nocturne	105
Face in the mirror	106
Committee hearings, 1952	107
Lil's monody	108
Black solstice	110
October	111
Storm outside, storm inside	112
The ceremony	113
Don plays Mozart	115
Woman with suitcase	117
Grand tour 1957	118

UNCOLLECTED POEMS

The well preserved man	123
Nightcrawler	125
Red brick monument	126
Dream of order at the carnival	128
How easy is forgetfulness	129
Eye contact	130
On technique	131
For a radical poet	132
The music wars	133
Between the end and the acceptance of the end	134
The air like stained glass cuts me	135

Wise dreaming	137
Man hung on himself	138
I vow to sleep through it	140
Midsummer night's stroll	142
Diptych	143
The diminishing addition	146
I have offended	148
In long drought	149
The correct method of worshipping cats	151
The name of that country is lonesome	152
Thou shalt not complain about anything I might have to fix	153
Always unsuitable	155

**From
THE TWELVE-SPOKED WHEEL FLASHING:
Poems of the middle Seventies**

The meaningful exchange

The man talks
the woman listens.

The man is a teapot
with a dark green brew
of troubles.
He pours into the woman.
She carries his sorrows away
sloshing in her belly.

The man swings off lighter.
Sympathy quickens him.
He watches women pass.
He whistles.

The woman lumbers away.
Inside his troubles are
snaking up through her throat.
Her body curls delicately
about them, worrying, nudging
them into some new meaningful shape
squatting now at the center of her life.

How much lighter I feel,
the man says, ready
for business.
How heavy I feel, the woman
says: this must be love.

Five thousand miles

Way past the curve of the earth
in a foreign country
you are sleeping, while it's twilight
here and Venus in its quarter phase
like a silver hook is taken
by a fishy grey cloud over Lake
Michigan. Through the earth
I should burrow to you like a mole.
I should wait for the moon to rise
and bounce off it, radar
to touch your sleeping face.

There you sleep and here
I walk wakeful and every day
is a calendar square like a prison yard
to pace. Every day is laid on
me and torn off like a bandage
on a slow dripping wound.

I burn with need
of you deep inside like a coal
mine that has caught fire
and smoulders far deep in the rock
away from the healing touch
of the rain, a slow poisonous
fire of wanting and waiting
that melts rocks
to tears of lava.

The summer invasion, and the fall

We liked her especially
because she was the color of sand
blending better with Cape grasses
than other ring-necked pheasants.
Today a hunter fired close by.

How I hate it every year
when the state releases them.
When the last of the summer traffic
has dwindled honking, when the fields
look clean again, they pick their way
with proud gait through
the bayberries, their soft plumage
dazzling, broad in the beam
as galleons under sail; how
pleased they are to be free.
They strut with the mourning
doves, the bluejays, the white
throated sparrows to the food
we put down. They do not know
they are exotica for hunters
to blow holes in. For a year
and a half we protected a pair.
The male had us trained
to feed them on demand. Ker-awk,
Ker-awk, he would summon us,
gargling gravel in his steeple neck.

A man came out of the marsh,
tore down the signs as he went
and shot the female in our yard.
We were glad the male seemed
to have escaped till we met
him on the road with his
leg shot off, flying
in crooked circles.

By October the summer tourist
garbage has sunk into the bushes. The Disney
puppies, the cuddly kittens
they got for their children like soft
ice cream cones to consume
have been thrown away pregnant,
starving. The cats haunt the narrow
lanes of Provincetown. I find
their ribbed hulks by the road.
The dogs run in packs on the beach
warring with seagulls. Few
go wild successfully, animals
disposed of like paper plates
after a picnic.

In November come beer cans heaped under
the oaks, spent shells, the brown trails
of deer with arrows in their bellies,
by the ponds the pellets of lead
the ducks will eat: the vermilion
hunters, national guardians
of a male mystique.

They polish their cars and campers;
do not dent them if you wish to live,
the tourists, the hunters. They oil
their lawn mowers at home, they
clean their shotguns and carry electric
knives, can openers, blankets.
They photograph the ocean
and drop plastic bottles in.
If something moves beautifully
through the grass it must be
bought in a package
raped, or shot.

Nothing you can have

February 28th and here
the first yellow crocuses
lift their cups to the sun,
the raspberries wait to be pruned:
all this morning I have been humming
a theme from Liszt
I cannot have heard since
I played it on the piano
at age seven: the sensuous honey
of melancholy veined
smoky with lust.

At eleven I sucked dreams
like sour lollipops
unsure what I wanted: now
smelly as an old hunting
jacket with blood and sweat
of many rutting seasons,
I still don't
know. It is not what
sex manuals describe
although the inability
to that well
shrivels the whole thing
like a cold draft
hitting a soufflé.

In my dreaming head
the lovers are dressed
in many layers: they talk
of other things with wit,
seldom of love. They fence.
Always something prevents
that consummation simple
as pissing. Gavottes,
minuets, strategies
complex as a protein molecule
bring them into short elegant
confrontations and whisk
them as quickly apart.

For three years I have
been stolid, content,
hard working, romantic
as a bulldozer moving manure.
February 28th, the sun
tingles, the air enters
my lungs busy as
a minnow flicking and darting.
Yet I droop, head
hanging a too heavy
sunflower, smiling,
sighing, hugging my arms.

At eleven I dreamed
of men who did not exist.
The same now. I know
what I can and cannot have.
The lovers who talk in my mind
are not yet born,
may never be. That dance
is one of equals,
bone by wish.

Spring will come with mud,
and I will slog in boots
to dig and plant my food.
This restlessness will hum
in my blood like a hive
preparing to swarm, and issue
on the still air of summer
buzzing and victorious
to change my life.

Archipelago

Seasonal, like a plant
that blooms in a desert.
For months nothing stirs
on baked cracked hills,
discards from a kiln.
Then after the soft rains
you can't see the ground
for the tangle of succulents
lush and twining.
Crowding gold cups gape
wide for the wind
scattering pollen
till the air shimmers.

We meet like dry sticks
scraping. A little sawdust,
claim grinding on claim,
the bang of hard ideas,
the rasp of opposing needs.

We meet like travelers
on an escalator in a busy
terminal, one riding up
while the other is lowered.
They set down the luggage
each is carrying and semaphore
wildly.

We meet like angler
and bucking bass and for
a moment before the line
snaps and the hook is
spat out in a cloud
of blood, a baleful
glancing look is exchanged.

We meet like Stanley
and Livingstone deep in the heart
of darkest fantasy, and as
one approaches brooding
on death and the other
on lecture tours and headlines,
the first words are spoken:
Did you pick up the mail?
What, you mean you didn't
bring my pills?

Yet always we do meet
as we grow older and more
ourselves, we meet
flashing in and out
of trouble, we meet
as the decades swell and buckle,
openly in cafés, clandestinely
on corners, at apartments
camped in overnight
scattered through ramshackle cities,
we meet and always
you are one of the friends
I think of in my life.

Yes, sometimes we meet
and it bursts into our own
season, fierce spring just born
butting, the sun young
and standing high and fiery
at the equinox, unscreened
by leaves, the buds still closed
but swelling, the wind strong
and salty. The dead
grass is pushed aside
by new blades coming
and every dusk the spring
peepers chorus joy from popping
throats deep in the marsh.
Season of plowed furrows, at night
the hunting owl, of seeds and mud,
the time of the hard wind
that quickens, the weightless
rasping caress of the wind.

The first salad of March

Thinnings of the rows,
Chinese cabbage, lettuce, sorrel,
cress; nipped ends of herbs
returning, mint and thyme;
violet leaves poking up
in clusters like armies
of teddy bears emerging
ears first from the earth;
the Egyptian onions that multiply
underground; the spears
of garlic shoots. The mixture
huddles, skimpy in the bowl.

The salad explodes in the mouth,
green roman candles.
It is succulent, dainty,
intense. It is crisp
as new money.
It lights up my blood
and urges fur from
the backs of my hands.
I want to roll in leaves
that are still lumps
on twigs. First salad
strong and fierce and plaintive:
love at age five. Spring
makes new the taste of lettuce
fresh as a tear.

Exodus

Out of cattle pen tenements
where the will to live fades out
like a forty watt bulb in the hallway's crotch;
out of streets rampant with proud metal
where men are mice at work
and slavering dogs afterward;
out of beds where women offer up
their only part prized whose name
is an insult and means woman here;
where anxiety yellows the air;
where greed paints over every window;
where defeat private as a worm
gnaws every belly,
we begin our slow halting exodus.
Egypt, you formed me from your clay.
I am a doll baked in your factory ovens,
yet I have risen and walked.

Like the Golem I am makeshift, lumbering.
I rattle and wheeze and my parts
are cannibalized T-birds and sewing machines,
mixers and wheelchairs, hair dryers.
My skin is the papier-maché of newspapers
cured with the tears of children
pregnant with hunger. My heart
is the stolen engine of an F-111.
My ligaments are knitting needles, hangers
recovered from the bodies of
self-aborted women. My teeth are military
headstones. I am the Golem.
Many breathed rage and hope into my
lungs, their roar
is my voice, their dreams
burning are my fuel.
They say nothing but a desert stretches
beyond, where the skulls of visionaries
are scoured by ants.

We have entered our Thirty Years' War
for a green place called the Country
of the Living. For two generations
we will be walking to a land we must build,
ourselves the bricks, the boards, the bridges,
in every face the map,
in every hand the highway.
We go clanking, stumbling forward, lurching.
Children born in that country
will play in the wreckage of our fears.

Ask me for anything else

Patience is dun-colored,
the mousy, the confusing
fall warbler that eats the worms,
the nourishment of beans and whole wheat,
the slow rain the crops
need that grows mold
on the mind.

Watson has patience and muddy
boots, not Holmes with his
cocaine needle. Old dogs
snore their patience.
Cats pace. Big cats
cut patience from the herd
and run it down panting
for hot breakfast.

Patience is a game you play
in a damp chilly cabin
while the river roars
and the path is too soggy
to hike out. Patience
is a tick waiting on a grass
blade for you or your dog.
Patience is the joy
of oysters.

Try me for energy, passion,
hard work, loyalty, hope,
but patience is the spider's
virtue, and I am
the glinting biting fly.

Patience is the library
angel, balancing water
in the air between cups.
I am the fiery one
leaping and gone.
How shall I wait
for you? I wring my hair
dry and the pebbles
of the minutes hit me
in the face. My hands
scrape the air.
I am empty with wanting,
not like a box
but like a tiger's belly.

What is permitted

How beautiful to be let
to stare into your eyes
from inches away, eyes of a shallow
sea with rock on the bottom
volcanic and jagged, rocks that slide
from the pass of scarlet poppies.

How beautiful to be permitted hours
of parentheses inside parentheses,
stories begun with so many details
they cannot end till three a.m.,
the talk stitching with fine silken
embroidery, the questioning with a child's
insistent thump, the angry mind
rooting up assumptions, the quick
pop to a different layer that leaves
me with my breath caught
in my throat like a kite in a tree.

How beautiful to hold you all
of a night, hour after hour,
tides of velvet splashing over,
under, pools of tawny feather,
flesh that hold sunlight
caught under the skin, to be given
you in me, to move with you, with
you out into the hot
rapids twisting and bobbing
till the river explodes.

How costly to be let into the halls
of your obsessions, buffeted by the moods
that shake you, the floors that
collapse in splinters, the stairways
that run backwards, the afternoons you will
do nothing but stare in the mirror
making faces, the doubts you swing,
bullwhips that threaten to
behead me, the times you walk through
me like fog, the times when you measure
each drop of affection like
an intravenous feeding solution.

What dance is this permitted
by the bearded gnomes of your fears,
two steps backward for each
step forward or is it
the other way round? Hopes
with rosy breast plumage still
build nests in my hair. Pain
puckers you yet I see the strength
there, the woman riding the crimson
lion through a field of flowers
and danger. My friend, of course
I will dance with you, how beautiful
that so much is permitted
when so much is feared.

A gift of light

Grape conserve from the red Caco vine
Robert and I planted five years ago:
rooted deep in the good dark loam
of the bottomland, where centuries
have washed the topsoil from the sandy
hill of pine and oak, whose bark
shows the scabs of fire.
Once this was an orchard on a farm.
When lilacs bloom in May I can find
the cellar hole of the old house.
Once this was a village of Pamet Indians.
From shell middens I can find their campground.

From the locust outside my window the fierce
hasty October winds have stripped the delicate
grassgreen fingernails. Winter is coming early.
The birds that go are gone, the plants retreating
underground, their hopes in tubers, bulb and seed.

The peaches, the tomatoes, the pears
glow like muted lanterns on their shelves. All
is put down for the winter except root crops
still tunneling under the salt hay mulch
we gathered at the mouth of the Herring River
as the sun kippered our salty brown backs.
Even the fog that day was hot as soup.
At evening when we made love
our skin tasted of salt and leather.

This year the autumn colors are muted.
Too much rain, wind tore the leaves loose
before they cured. Tonight I will be with Robert,
tomorrow with you. I braid my life in its
strong and muted colors and I taste my love
in me this morning like something harsh
and sweet, like raw sugarcane I chewed in Cuba,
fresh cut, oozing sap.

On those Washington avenues that resemble
emperor-sized cemeteries vast Roman mausoleum
after mausoleum where Justice and Health
are budgeted out of existence for the many, men
who smell of good cologne are pushing pins
across maps. It is time to attack the left
again, it is time for a mopping up
operation against those of us who opposed
their wars too soon, too seriously, too long.
It is time to silence the shrill voices
of women whose demands incommode men
with harems of illpaid secretaries, men
for whom industries purr, men who buy death wholesale.
Today some are released from prison and others
are sucked in. Those who would not talk
to grand juries are boxed from the light
to grow fungus on their brains and those
who talked received a message, it is time
to talk again.

I try hard to be simple in loyalty.
I try hard to remember always
to ask for whom what is done is done.
Who gets and who loses? Who pays
and who rakes off the profit? Whose
life is shortened? Whose heat
is shut off? Whose children end
up shooting up or shot in the streets?

I try to remember to ask simple questions.
I try to remember to love my friends and fight
my enemies. But their faces are hidden
in the vaults of banks, their names are inscribed
on the great plains by strip mining and you can
only read the script from Mars. Their secret
wills are encoded in the computers that mind
nuclear submarines armed with the godheads
of death. They enter my blood invisible
as the Sevin in the water that flows
from the tap, in strontium 90 in milk.

You are part friend and part enemy: you
are part guerrilla and part prison guard.
I hold you in my arms, but beer commercials
have programmed your fantasies, the Bank
of Boston has a lien on your love. Sometimes
you care more to control me than for winning
this lifelong war. If I am your colony
you different only in scale from Rockefeller.
I want to trust you the way I want
to drink water when my tongue is parched,
the way I want to crouch by a fire
when I have hiked miles through snowy woods.
I want to trust you as much as I want to live.

Let no one doubt, no onlookers, no heirs
of our agonies, how much I have loved
what I have loved. Flying back
from Washington,, I saw the air steely
bright out to the huge bell of horizon.
I leaned against the plane window, cheek
to the plastic, crooning to see the curve
of the Cape hooking out in the embrace
of the water, to see the bays, the tidal
rivers, the intricate web of marshes,
the body of this land like beautiful
lace, like a fraying bronze net cast
on the glittering fish belly of the sea.

I dig my hands into this hillside wrist
deep, my nails are stubby and under them
is my own land's dirt. I bring you
this gift of grape conserve from shelves
of summer sun bottled like glowing lights
I hope we survive free and contentious to taste,
as I bring myself, my mouth opening
to taste you, my hands that know how
to touch you, belly and back and cunt,
history and politics. I bring you trouble
like a hornet's nest in a hat
to roost on your head. I bring you
struggle and trouble and love
and a gift of grape conserve to melt
on your tongue, red and winey,
the summer sun within like soft jewels
passing and strong and sweet.

Short season

Past timberline alpine
flowers tinge the slope
making clumps some
feet apart in the red
volcanic ash.
Against the rusty scree
the goldfinch-bright stonewort
sprawls, the scarlet
paintbrush, moss campion
at the trickle of the glacier,
the uplifted blue lupine
intense as alcohol flames
wavering in the sun.

Not long ago lava
gushed here killing
everything. The mountain
sleeps fitfully, wakes me
at three in the morning
stirring like a huge
bear in hibernation.
The slowed heart does not
seem to beat but it does.
Spring will come for
the great red bear under
the ice cap, under the sheer crags.

Flowers are between disasters.
They happen in the quick
summer, avidly pushing their organs
into the pure sugar rush
of the sun, sucking the rain,
coming in pollen gustily.
But a volcano seen from far
away is a red and gold flower.
After the earthquake,
the explosion, the rivers
of magma, the mountain
is reborn coned
like a perfect breast.

The trouble is I am too small
to take comfort. My eye
stops on the flower, my
life beats in the moment
when the petals unfold,
when my thighs open
and both our bodies
quake and still.

Ghosts

The skin falls like leaves
in slow motion, I know it,
is sifted and shifted
by the wind like a dune.
The skin that knew you
seven years back
has sluffed and grown part
of another, a Jersey cow,
an oak tree, a crow.

The years wear holes in us;
what looks solid as sheet
metal, one morning the glass
face of the next building
peers through. Theories, rhetoric
fade like a Mail Pouch ad
on an old barn, but the structure
stands firm while the winds
howl through the necessary cracks.

What lives of the woman who
loved you? The fears that twittered
stripping me bare and bony
have risen in a shrill flock
and settled in younger women.
I worry about money
but rarely about my face;
responsibilities hang at my tits
squealing and fat as baby pigs.

Your ghost curls floating in the closed
waters of dream. Your mouth
moves on my throat in the dark,
my hands exactly form your back,
unscalded by the blood of our parting.
I wake trembling in a body you never
touched, while past the curve of the earth
you sleep. Time thickens you.
On the street would I know your face?

The new novel

I wade into you.
Oh how fat you are.
You want to eat me up.

That is, I guess, how men perceive women:
the way you appear to engulf me
as I invent you.

Through spring and summer and winter
and summer again you
will leach my dreams wan.
I will racket thin nights
through your skeletal rooms
still open to the unfamiliar sky
where ominous green moons
swim through constellations
scratched on my lids.

I will secrete you daily
at length to hang spent
while you crawl from me,
the chrysalis the butterfly abandons.
What remains to me
but to become a caterpillar
yet again:
the best part of me
locked in those
strange paper boxes.

Women of letters

I used to write twenty-two-page-
single-spaced letters to friends,
keeping illegible carbons, not once
in a decade but every week.
Now sometimes I get such letters
from women I don't know, now when
I dictate one-paragraph letters
to lovers.

Somehow I've lost faith in letters,
no longer believe in my biography.
Lost the faith that if I explain everything
love will come in the return mail,
insured, registered, hot
for my signature.

Women dyeing the air with desperation,
women weaving like spiders from the gut
of emptiness, women
swollen with emotion, women with words
piling up in the throat like fallen leaves
to rot there, impacting;

women complaining, telling, retelling
agonies like amber worry beads, sores
like the beads of rosaries, click click,
click click, death, desertion, prison,
neglect, hunger, protestations of
genius and abasement twined
like strands of rotting rope,
I remember, I remember it all.

It is me at fifteen, at nineteen at
twenty-four or twenty-eight, casting
letters on the face of the dark waters
to float out with the sewage, tearing
bits of small flesh to attract the fluttering birds,
shipping off my dreams, my opinions,
my terrors to people who did not
bother to read them. Who wants to get
a twenty-two-page-single-spaced letter
from a crazy ranting poet-ess housed
in a rotting molar on Wilson Avenue, Chicago,
with a stench of poverty like overripe cheese.
Into the mailslot and out to the super
along with the Sunday funnies
and coffee grounds.

I wrote letters instead of making
speeches, instead of reviewing books,
instead of climbing Mount
Washington, instead of giving poetry
readings at universities, instead of
flying on a business trip to the Coast,
instead of living with the three people who love me,
instead of raising apples and potatoes,
instead of buying a car, instead of
buying a machine gun, instead of
having books I wrote finally published.

Not that they all want to write, except
that print seems to make visible
what others walk through like smog,
the radiation of pain, of need, of identity
screaming like a cat in heat to deaf ears.

After Phyllis wrote *Women and Madness*
they brought the mail in boxes. Boxes upon boxes
like moving day, each full of bloody hanks of hair,
gobbets of flesh, bits of charred skin.
What shall I do with them? She asked us,
drinking gin from a tumbler. *If I answer them
it will take the rest of my life, and how
should I answer them?* Catharine and Martha and I
took each a handful and all evening
we wrote answers, practical, pragmatic (see
your local women's center, clinic, Legal Aid,
send for this booklet, that set of instructions
— plugs, Band-Aids, masking tape).
When we had finished typing, we too got drunk
and still there were more boxes carried up
in the morning, boxes singing
like mad linnets of pain's needle.

Does no one out there listen?
Yet I remember riding with my mother on buses
 in Detroit, and I would be so embarrassed I would
tug at her hand, because always
some woman would stare into her face
and begin to tell, click click,
click click, death, desertion, prison,
neglect, hunger, and I think of all the bartenders
drying glasses behind all the bars, and all the psychiatrists
whose clocks tell money by seconds, and all
the letters thrashing like stranded gasping fish
in mailbags everywhere.

Stop writing letters! Stop! We will
come together instead. Each three
will prove that the fourth exists,
will listen, will look, that gift
of open eyes and ears greater than charity.
Let the letters mate like flounder
in the secret bags and their roe ferment.
It is each other only
who can save us with gentle attention
and make us whole.

From LIVING IN THE OPEN
Poems of the early Seventies

The token woman

The token woman gleams like a gold molar in a toothless mouth.

The token woman arrives like a milkbottle on the stoop
coming full and departing emptied.

The token woman carries a bouquet of hothouse celery
and a stenographer's pad; she will take
the minutes, perk the coffee, smile
like a plastic daisy and put out
the black cat of her sensuous anger
to howl on the fence all night.

A fertility god serves a season
then is ritually dismembered
yet the name, the function live on:
so she finds the shopping lists
of exiled women in her coat pockets.

The token woman stands in the Square of the Immaculate
Exception blessing pigeons from a blue pedestal.
The token woman falls like a melon seed
on the cement: why has she no star shaped yellow flowers?
The token woman is placed like a scarecrow
in the longhaired corn: her muscles are wooden.
Why does she ride into battle on a clothes horse?
The token woman is a sandbag plugging
the levee: shall the river
call her sister as the flood waters rage?

The token woman is a black Chicana fluent in Chinese
who has borne 1.2 babies
(not on the premises, no child care provided)
owns a Ph.D., will teach freshman English
for a decade and bleach your laundry
with tears, silent as a china egg.
Your department orders her from a taxidermist's catalog
and she comes luxuriously stuffed with goosedown
able to double as sleeping
or punching bag.

Another woman can never join her,
help her, sister her, tickle her
but only replace her to become her
unless we make common cause,
unless she grows out, one finger of a hand,
the entering wedge, the runner
from the bed of rampant peppermint
as it invades the neat clipped turf
of the putting green.

The clearest joy

The clearest joy
is the ceasing of great pain.
When the iron bell rises from the head,
when the clanging shock subsides along the nerves,
when the body slides free
like a worm from a hook,
how the putrid city air
bubbles in the lungs.
Light glides in honey over the eyes.
The austere ceiling is made of meringue.
The body uncoils, uncoils
wonderfully empty like a lily.
Breathing is dancing.
Dumbly and wholly
like the basil plant on the sill
I lift my nose into the sun.

Make me feel it

My head is full of folded linen.
My nerves are the bones of smelt.
If the hearts of the enemies of womankind
were served on plates with sauce vinaigrette
I would eat them and belch.
If the amber bodies of lively sensual boys
came leaping through my bed in dolphin schools
I would fuck them and yawn.
I am an unbaited mousetrap.
The fungus of boredom coats my tongue.
Friends step over me like a crack.
My head is a waiting room in Dayton Ohio
where people in galoshes drowse under a stalled clock.

I need an old friend to drop dead so I may weep.
I need a good fighter to be murdered by the CIA so I may care.
The old sores are covered with scar tissue.
Once in Iowa City, Iowa in a friend's room
I found in his desk notes for an elegy
to be written on the death of Pound, his favorite poet.

A good thunderstorm of anger would galvanize me.
Ah, for a touch of the power coming through.
My lady, I am your hammer: make me ring against stone.
Mama, pick me up again and wear me,
I am your weapon.
My poetry and my politics have come unstuck.
Goddess, I am down to the brief hassles of the body,
the nerves struck like kitchen matches on the dark,
my wit which wants to diddle itself in the stacks of libraries.

Sweet mama, a life is as far as I can walk on it.
I have been lazy and lax,
I have been wanton and wobbly,
but take me up. Strop me.
Frighten the too easy wits out
till I leap and chatter and flash green,
let your hairy lightning blast me open and quaking.
I fear nothing like this silence
filled with the satisfied nibbling of myriad teeth
of the little appetites.

Sage and rue

This afternoon I have been cutting herbs for vinegar:
the spicy warmth of basil lifting raggedy spikes,
the pinedark ferns and yellow umbrels of dill,
the rampant dense mints,
the coarse grassy leaves of tarragon
ruffled with dead stubs at the base.
In that harsh acid, the savor will be trapped and held.

I have been cutting herbs to dry in the shed.
Making potpourri and tea for the winter,
picking over withered leaves from the racks.
The tedium of plucking into bottles soothes me.
My fingers smell of thyme and lemon verbena.

Though the flowers of chives are starry pink purple,
most herbs are weeds, flowers small and habit sprawling.
Bees hang on them, drunk with odors.
Other insects pass by, except jade-striped caterpillars
on the dill and the fennel who menace me with short
sticky horns erupting matter that would dissuade me
if I meant to eat them.

Herbs give sparingly. They will not sustain
you but render palatable what does.
They will heal, they will soothe, they will play
on your chemistry ringing small changes,
pleasure you in the bath and scent your clothes.

Asking little and slowly giving what no one needs
they thrive in poor soil under the blast of the sun.
Servants of witches, they draw cats.
Under the lovage my Persian washes a paw,
my Siamese is lounging debauched in the nepenthe,
                                              while an orange
stranger stalks a toad through the parsley and lilies.

I brush the rosemary with my scissors and sieve.
The small things of this world are sufficient and magical.
I praise the green power of fresh herbs
and the fragrant ghosts of dried, the redolent vinegars.
I praise things that remain themselves
though cut off from what fed them, through transformations.

River road, high toss

In the reeds the blue
heron stalks, titled great
for his height, his antiquity,
that cool old lift of the heart
when he flies over the water
on ragged sails of wing
his big feet tucked but dragging.

The black ducks are maneuvering
in flotillas. On the narrow
rim at low tide are carved
the neat paw prints
of the raccoon where she washed her food.
The yellow-breasted chat
chucks from the briar.
Past the bridge where the
Herring River narrows
the sweetest and the
thorniest blackberries grow
in languid arches studded with spikes
trussed with long berries dripping juice
like a parable of pleasure and pain.

Paradise Hollow

Follow the old ruts,
circle the freshly fallen pine
broken in the last high wind,
stopping to free the young
sapling to rise again.
Follow the big friendly hands
like children's drawings,
of the sassafras. Filé gumbo.
Follow the ax cut path
narrower than your hips
through the labyrinth
of trees toppled years ago
in fire, the midden heap
of a farmhouse, daylilies,
broken plates of blue willow,
shells and rusted plow:
now the sumac tangles
wild and lacy over bones.

At the core of the hollow
the brook trickles
through a red maple swamp.
In winter we can hop
from mossy gray hummock to hummock
when the briar dies back.

Follow the brook to its source,
a spring in a meadow
still grassy from the
invisible house. The old apple
trees tall now as the black locusts
offer their gnarled and wormy
fruit like memories.

Kneeling here, I feel good

Sand: crystalline children
of dead mountains.
Little quartz worlds
rubbed by the wind.

Compost: rich as memory,
sediment of our pleasures,
orange rinds and roses and beef bones,
coffee and cork and dead lettuce,
trimmings of hair and lawn.

I marry you, I marry you.
In your mingling under my grubby nails
I touch the seeds of what will be.
Revolution and germination
are mysteries of birth
without which
many
are born to starve.

I am kneeling and planting.
I am making fertile.
I am putting
some of myself
back in the soil.
Soon enough
sweet black mother of our food
you will have the rest.

16 in 53

Your elephant adolescence in sandlots Brooklyn:
it sloshes like a washtub with nostalgia.
Heroes stalked in your attic dragging chains of words.
In the coalbin you lifted weights
your belly pink as strawberry ice cream.
You counted body hairs like daisies
foretelling love/notlove/notlove.
Pillows of snow, girls melted leaving damp rings.
At night a toad big as a gas storage tank,
you brooded over Flatbush muttering warts.
You lay in bed becoming snotgreen Dedalus:
you would not wash
wanting your Jewish mother to threaten you with rosaries,
excommunication, the hierarchic ashes of creaky saints.
In bed you were secretly thin with scorn
while your parents doted and fed you stuffed cabbage,
while outside the frowzy neighbors
browsing on newspapers and growing mad
with the cold dim light of television flickering in their eyes
danced, danced in the streets
for the burning to death
of Julius and Ethel Rosenberg.

The big one

My dear, you are a giant burr
caught in the world's short hairs.
You are a backporch floppy chair with stuffing
leaking out of your belly and all buttons gone
and when I plunk down
a cloud of dust hides me
and I rise up smelling of old dog.
My dear, you are a leaky red hot-water bottle.
You are a telephone that does not answer
unless I bash its head against the wall.
You are a bright yellow rose
the size of a boxer's fist.
This poem could go on as you must,
on through the marshes of your ennui.
You must get on with planting pits
in the bottom half of milk cartons and old galoshes,
squeezing poems out of the toothpaste tube of your guts,
crystallizing the best thoughts of all
out of the absolute zero
of the lonely night ice of vision.

There is no known way to tickle a clam

You say, things are getting better between us.
You shout that over your shoulder
as you race down an Up escalator
and out through a subway tunnel.
A train head on would scare you less than I
as I circle waving handkerchiefs and daisies.
You draw up your knees and turn clam.
You think I want to steal your soggy pearls.
Snap: you snip off my finger.
Do you think you could be eaten
whole? In parts? For breakfast?
You cannot remember who I am: fragments
break off and float loose
like something rotting under water.
Slimecold suspicion pumping through
washes the slight web of affection away like waste.
Your shell builds involution upon involution
and you are closing down outer chambers of your mind.
Total defense
implies a dream of total surrender
but my hands are not tools for opening shells
and it was never my intention
to consume you.

Two higher mammals

Each anniversary we share still
the attempt to grow, a politics
much too large for us
in which we rattle
wizened seeds in a beautiful gourd.
Even our cats are fussy eaters.
If only we were furry green chimps,
giant roseate thinking amoebae,
blue humanoids with quivering antennae
peaceful in instinct
and good to the core like bananas.

But we are woman and man,
other and murderous brother,
predators in whose fried brains
sputter all the raddled static
and greedy gobble of our race.
Faces of bored losers
yawn in our bones.

Loving leaves stretch marks.
Thinking clearly still hurts.
To be good for anything
is furious struggle
wrestling like dinosaurs
not only with the enemy
but with our own tough
and armored tails, weights
we drag behind.

Beautiful weeper

Come under the willow
tree in the fall,
its yellow cataract
of languor: hair
of lady shuddering.
In the spring
the wands will brighten
early as forsythia.
Willow, willow by the water
your roots creep
into pipes and drains
to clog them
with your secret vigor.
Willow, willow shivering,
you look ethereal to survive,
you droop for a living
while underground your vast
root system thrives.
I want to be as little like you
as they will let me
except for your energy
striving for water to live,
willow,
sister willow.

The legacy

Bury that family grandeur
of mink in mothballs,
rotting marble. Stop
lugging through furnished rooms
ancestral portraits
in a deck of marked cards.
Toss out those wroughtiron crutches.
Success like an incubus
visits your bed.
Nothing you do
will ever be enough.
You cannot win a prize
grand enough to ransom
your mother's youth.
The incense of those years
one by one guttered out
faint light, faint heat
chokes me in your room,
smothers you as you sleep
dreaming in hand-me-downs,
while dead women's wishes
like withered confetti
snow through your head.

The consumer

My eyes catch and stick
as I wade in bellysoft heat.
Tree of miniature chocolates filled with liqueur,
tree of earrings tinkling in the mink wind,
of Bach oratorios spinning light from discs,
tree of Thailand silks murmuring changes.
Pluck, eat and grow heavy.
From each hair a wine bottle dangles.
A toaster is strung through my nose.
An elevator is installed in my spine.
The mouth of the empire
eats onward though the apple of all.
Armies of brown men
are roasted into coffee beans,
are melted into chocolate,
are pounded into copper.
Their blood is refined into oil,
black river oozing rainbows
of affluence.
Their bodies shrink
to grains of rice.
I have lost my knees.
I am the soft mouth of the caterpillar.
People and landscapes are my food
and I grow fat and blind.

A short dark turning

The full moon on the winter solstice
darkness at midafternoon
and the sea rising,
the gray creep of water through ditches
into lowlands and pasture,
the tentacles of the sea penetrate
where I have never seen water over the land.
The river brims
slapping the boards of the bridge.

Rain has come down wet month by month.
Other years, we counted raindrops like pearls,
we watched clouds scoot over on their way to the sea.
This is the year of the mushroom,
potato head sprouting in the path,
shelves crusting the fencepost,
toadstool erect between wet leaves.
Marshes lick their edges. Basements fill.

Not human justice but that of the earth,
the circle of all intertwined,
persuades me as Nixon bombs the dikes,
seeds the clouds with silver iodide
and nudges the typhoon off course for Hanoi,
great balances tip.
The wettest year since measurement began here.
 Now the sea runs high on sodden land.
This is the season of low energy and a stingy sun.
The sky rattles old newspapers.

On Vietnam at the winter solstice
more bombs rain
than ever fell on people.
The wind is wet tonight off the gulf stream
with large warm drops like blood.
I am lettering a poster about the war.
For a moment I can't remember what year this is, dying.
A new year will be born from the waning moon
to carry hope like a tallow candle
in the bloody rain.
The sea is still rising.

For a Brazilian 'Bandit'

You are
no stronger than me:
your back hurt.
I lay down to show you
my morning exercises,
prayers of my body to survive,
the slow stretching
that strengthens my weak back.
When you tried
you shook with effort.

You are
no larger than me;
when I embraced you on parting
my arms doubled on your back.
I could lift you to my knees.
We could trade clothes.

The rifle is your weapon,
the typewriter mine.
Your way is harder.
My way is fatter.

You are no stronger,
no taller.

As I read the newspapers
I will remember.
Every time it is necessary
to do something hard
I will remember:

Your back is weak
your hands are small
your breasts are low and apart
your ankles are delicate
like mine.
We are fighting the same battle
and you also love roses,
write poems.

The box

You are with me but gone.
Your skin grows bark. It
does not want to be translucent
to my touch.

I am a problem; you will solve me.
I am a demand; you will cancel me.
I am a shortage; you will audit me.

If I am green you crave purple.
If I am warm you sweat.
If I am round you bounce off.
The tides of my dreams
ruffle your sleep.
My loud needs slice like
helicopters through your air.

Sometimes you confuse me
with air, with water, with pollen,
the medium you live in,
with the clock of the heart
that runs slowly down,
with time that files
every hill flat.

To try cannot mean going backward.
The past is stored in our bones.
Do you want to walk onward
toward that blank wall?
Now we walk at the wall very fast
holding hands and trying to act as if
we believe in an opening.
If we come through the stone
we come through
in an unknown place.

January Thaw

Six days
narrow as razors
yet wide enough
as that single bed
we slept on, tangled.

Deep enough to free fall
twined, dancing
through that huge temporary
space, wind whistling
the land turning
like the hands of a clock
the sun far below us.

Though dead winter
the chickadees are calling
as they do in spring
fe-ver, fe-ver rising,
descending sweetly.

A January thaw, country
roads turned chocolate pudding
our boots with sucking sounds
clambering over the still-
intact oak leaves
pages of an old diary
an old year
thrown off.

The air is Chablis.
The stinking Huron
we called the Urine, rages
in its ordered dirty banks
like a mountain stream.
The sun teases my arms.
Your mouth makes me drunk.
My body opens to a purple crocus.
Your hands on my back descend
a perfect scale.

You there, me here.
I bleed a slow
electricity of pain.
Six lean days
flashing like razors
and gone.

Phases of the sun

July, full fat July
sweet as honeydew melon
cool breeze skimming foam off the sea
sun licking my skin
still as a cocoon on a branch
I lie, shaping invisible changes
in my head veined blue
as a cheese with dreams.

I need to be alone
yet missing you, it's
a thorn of pure sugar
piercing me.

A rhythm of here and gone
parting and closing
sliding shut and letting go,
our mating isn't a house
not even a trailer.

It's a path lit
by candles, one
for each bed we share,
votive offerings to the
proud eight-armed red
earth gods we are together.

Lies

1.

Always I feel it
bloating like a tumor
a weight, a shape
brushing my thighs
as I wade into sleep.

The water is warm like my blood
flat as a kitchen table.
My face dances there
in sun circles.
The water is a caress.
Then a fin breaks the surface
coming fast.

2.

You say I hate lying
because I want to be a child
holding my mother's hand.
You say no one needs to know
more than she needs.
You say, what is truth then?
Does it come in a package?
You say confession
is false orgasm.
You say feeding people part
of yourself is an attempt to bribe
them into love, you
there in the mirror.

3.

What I retain of my year with him
are the lies time has
filtered out in its coarse sieve
nuggets of fool's gold.
Every few weeks washes out another
to drop in my palm
bright, hard, worthless
yielding nothing but its own
nature, a dead end.

Strange to be left with his lies,
overnight constructions, the façades
of skyscrapers thrown up in panic,
Potemkin villages of the mind
forbidding the intimacy
he saw as invasion.
His best energy went into defense.
It is a poor creature like a slug
who builds the cathedrals of conch shell.

4.

Fear turns me nimble.
Chilled by coercion I flash
words, I glint facts, an acrobat
one-handed on top of a pike
juggling plates, balls and footstools
while sword dancing
with my toes and teeth.
One gauge of weakness
is to be forced to lie to a judge,
parent, caseworker, cop or other
thug of power.

5.

I live in a crazy house
with the blinds drawn tight
and the doors wide open.

Honesty is a compulsion swinging a
heavy sword like loving
like poetry itself.
I give too much importance to words
and my words define me.
I am always becoming words
that walk off as strangers.
Words, words, you sit, vultures eyeing my body.
You wait for my fat heart.
Isn't it enough that I spew all this paper?
What do I owe you
that I must try to love with words?
Sand in a sieve.

Lies catch in the teeth and rot there.
The truth goes down like water,
little taste, but
the stuff we're made of.

For Inez Garcia

A woman's honor has been the possession
of her keeper, like the speed
of a race horse or the bloodline
of a pedigreed bitch, that no other man spoil
his wife, nor his ox, nor his ass.
Men have groomed their honor, embellishing it
in golden embroideries of legend heavy as iron gates;
have elaborated strict rituals of honor
armored in hierarchies of pain,
the samurai carving in his bowels and belly
a slow deep cross with his own blade.
The knight's noblesse oblige assumes the ignoble
obliged to bow and scrape and whine
if it please your honor, thanking your honor, please,
mercy! As fear rises like mud in the throat.

But what of my honor: Where do I draw
that red line, the perimeter of my will?
Am I everyman's urinal?
What does it mean to say No?
What does it mean to say No to superior force?

The man's body is a weapon and the woman's
a target. We are trained to give way.
give in, keep quiet, make peace.
Speak to the rapist nicely, speak softly
and reasonably, assure him you have
his best interests at heart. Kiss the knife.
Perhaps he will not injure you too much.

Perhaps he will not kill you today.
Perhaps the injury will close to scar tissue.
Perhaps you will forget to be afraid
the rest of your life, perhaps you will forget
what it is like to be used as a public toilet,
torn open like the throat
of a slaughtered calf.
Perhaps it would be good to open him.

To say Yes one must be able
to say No: No to the other,
the invader, the violator,
no. How does one say No
to superior force? The city is bombed
flat and taken, the field is pillaged
and burnt, the house is gutted. The woman
lies in the dust with her mouth
and cunt bleeding.

She rises. She rises to seize
the weapon and say again No
in blood. The only No that holds
is written in letters of bone.
Power accepts no lesser currency.

You cannot smoke your honor, you cannot
show it to your caseworker, you cannot
pay it in the supermarket for a can of beans.
Like freedom it doesn't exist
unless you make it. A woman's honor
is rooted in being able to say yes,
to say no and make each stick fast,
that ghostly will that rises in us
from the prone corpse of our passivity
like a resurrection, naked and thin and strange,
spirit of the responsible will
walking and talking from the grave
of the body that ate the child
that swelled into the woman, that now gives birth
to her own new holy being that carries high
a sword, a torch, a rifle. There is no
holiness without terror, no will
without responsibility and consequence,
no entire person without boundaries,
without doors that open and close
and the will to guard what goes
out and what comes in.

Let Inez Garcia, Joan Little become
two faces in a crowd of women, an army
each defending her body, defending her sister,
defending the frail ghost of the new whole
conscious self struggling to stand upright
and walk, like a nine year old child.

HARD LOVING
Poems from the late Sixties

Easy

How easy it is to be happy
you say sometimes,
chocolate afternoons,
the summer sun on our bodies,
rarely a whole night
big as the biggest pumpkin.
We can eat it all.
Playing in the streets
I am shy
because you are so beautiful
women want to attack me
with envy
with purses and nails.
I should whisper to them
no, no, he is not mine
we are guests together
but still, how easy
easy as butter
easy and silk and honey
to turn and touch you
you, sometimes
when you really look back at me
when you really see me
and be happy
at once, like eating icecream.

Joy as a point

One night in January
In the middle of sore times
I lay in your arms
too taut with joy
to douse in sleep
In the morning brown eggs
you sang in the kitchen come
if you want to, come
and the night and the morning
a tough tall raggedy flower
a flag red hollyhock
sprung from snow and asphalt
you leapt in my arms
I danced in your skin
the sun stood still
at the pole of night
we knocked like balloons
against the ceiling
all the night and the morning
burning but softly
without smoke or ash
bursting in rough bloom
out of ice and asphalt
pomegranate red
one January night.

The fisherman

You are trawling with a fine net in your depths.
Up they come and spill on the varnished deck
and their phosphorescence dims
and their colors begin to fade,
shy creatures who swell and burst,
tenuous flimsy beasts that shrivel and dry up
till all die gasping.
See! You address the stinking pile,
you are not real.

Your eyes are hard, and other surprises

Will the white sun rise?
Throat packed with salt and rockdust.
My cactus eyes.

Someone has twisted my shadow.
Small and smaller, hunchbacked it drags.
Where will it go?

In closets I plead my case,
in toilet stalls, in furnace rooms.
My smiling face

unpeels in hanging strips.
Words that foam and dry and harden
tear my lips.

Hey my enemy, whose hate
sleets on me, do the hairs of your belly
remember my sweat?

I still feel you

Like a fishbone in my throat
or one of your hairs that used to catch in my teeth
a piece of iron is travelling through my muscles,
a bit of jagged iron,
an end of harpoon or a broken hook.
Now it sticks as I catch my breath.
Now as I run downstaires it bites my instep.
Now it is tunnelling through my belly.
It leaks a slow rust into the blood,
a sad dark orange taste on my tongue
acid but meek.
Blindly this mental remnant wanders in me
as you did, blindly taking the easiest way
in or out
whether you found an opening,
orifice or old wound,
or had to cut one.

Missing person

When you are off in another city
that city is lit up like a gold tooth,
a whistle blowing orange in the corner of my mind.
the earth is lopsided toward Boston.
People in the street swarm up invisible hills.
I am walking crooked:
my head leans north.
Nothing is uglier than a beige telephone
hiding you inside
squat and smug and miserly
with the dial of a combination lock on a safe.
Sleepwalking, I dream of a city that clucks like a hen
covering you with feathery smoke and barnred houses.
Stalled between day and night,
numbed by exhaust fumes, dulled by waiting,
time without you I walk through a tunnel
where anxieties drip and stain the walls
and fans beat the air like drowning swimmers.
A tunnel is between, a tunnel ends,
I cannot get lost in a tunnel
but not until the last turn
can I see the light.

Song of the nudge

There are eight people in this room.
I am loving five of them
whether they like it or not and often they don't,
being hopped by an electric windmill with cowbells,
a rain of salamanders and feather beds and overripe onions.
My loving is a sweaty tango with a python
among the marshmallow bushes, I know it.
Today two of these people filmed a girl with a smile
trying to give dollars or flowers to passers-by
who ducked their heads and hustled on.
There is no love without its coercion,
there are no gifts without taxes.
Nothing belongs to me except my hands
and I go around trying to give them away.
A spare hand in the house, nasty, curious as a monkey,
you couldn't keep it in a cage. What would it eat?
It would probably break things.
It is probably better to lock the door.

This is a poem for you

This is a poem for me
when the clock of my muscles runs down,
when my brain is a sponge oozing vinegar,
when I cover the mirror to lock in the ghosts.
This is a poem for you
after they have broken our heads and bodies,
when we are grey numbers in grey prisons,
when we are scattered in dusty cafes in dead-end freight ports.
Remember when we were most beautiful not by twos,
never in formless plenaries or mumbly caterpillar meetings
but in small high holy groups shifting like starfish.
In odds and end rooms off insecticide corridors,
in dim lofts among lumber
we dance and touch in pulsing circles.
Our faces rise up soft and blurred with laughter.
Our faces float jagged with sudden wanting.
We shimmer with sweat.
We are playing out our knowledge of each other.
We are asking riddles with our hands
and solving them with our hips.
We are a soft clumsy organism.
Music blows through the long tangled pelt,
the red mouth is open to roar and taste,
the eyes are wide and bright and moist,
the paws are raised.

Reopening

Somewhere in the tunnel of winter
the machines of hope turned off and the air went bad.
Too many lies have been handed you like canapés to eat.
Each defeat was small, each endurable one by one by one
till a mountain of dead roaches blocked your way.
You turned aside crying. Nothing matters except people.
You thought your love a gift friends would receive gladly
like a blank cheque,
but each asked only, What do you want for this?
Slowly you closed down to a charged coil of pain.
Then the spark leapt the gap at me, burning.
We fought and ripped till the blood broke through the skin
and the nerves went off like sirens
and the old and new wounds lit up in the dark like eyes.
Slowly we gathered each other's dismembered body,
knit the mangled limbs,
closing each wound with mouth and fingers and hair,
a slow underwater dance in the other's eyes.
Love, my love, my love you have come back
but it is a planet with different colored sea and skies,
strange bright birds to sing, and new sweet and bitter fruit.
Healing, we are a new animal with new instincts and strengths
and nothing feels or tastes the same
except our love.

Rain falls on Ioannina

Grey clouds sink.
All day from my hotel room
I watch the grey lake rise.
I rub and blow on inkstained fingers
patient as that wading stork.
Fog creeps in the window.
Smoke spools out.
From the cracked egg
of looted synagogue
weeds sprout in the rain.
In the glass and concrete orphanage
girls are learning to weave rugs
to sell to tourists.
It is not so bad, they say.
The soldier said the same,
hitchhiking toward his village
of rocks and gnarled shepherds,
about the army. The equipment
is new and American.
The army is a major industry
as under the Turks,
as under the Germans.
I am American and a tourist.
I am learning something about wet
and grey and bad.

To grow on

The first chickyellow probes of sun
fluffy with mopdust
touch the windows.
Nothing here is quite
smooth or whole.
The pipes weep rust,
boards sag and heave,
plaster sighs into dust
and from the ceiling tatter
winsome stalactites
of paint.

On the ledges
old paint blisters into maps.
Chips of pretty paint
snow on the crib.
Paint, the landlord's friend,
holds up the walls.
All winter children peck it.

In the first cornsyrup pools of sun
small fingers uncoil
like germinating beans.
Fingers: test tubes
for that simple chemistry:
sun activates the lead
winter's swallowed drifts
whose tired colours now
run through the blood.

Death blooms with the
suburban hyacinths.
Even spring
charges a little more
to the poor.

The morning half-life blues

Girls buck the wind in the grooves toward work
in fuzzy coats promised to be warm as fur.
The shop windows snicker
flashing them hurrying over dresses they cannot afford:
you are not pretty enough, not pretty enough.

Blown with yesterday's papers through the boiled coffee morning
they dream of the stop on the subway without a name,
the door in the heart of the grove of skyscrapers,
that garden where we nestle to the teats of a furry world,
like in mounds of peony eating grapes,
and need barter ourselves for nothing,
not by the hour, not by the pound, not by the skinful,
that party to which no one will give or sell them the key
though we have all thought briefly we had found it
drunk or in bed.

Black girls with thin legs and high necks stalking like herons,
plump girls with blue legs and green eyelids
                              and strawberry breasts,
swept off to be frozen in fluorescent cubes,
the vacuum of your jobs sucks your brains dry
and fills you with the ooze of melted comics.
Living is later. This is your rented death.
You grasp at specific commodities and vague lusts
to make up, to pay for each day
which opens like a can and is empty, and then another,
afternoons like dinosaur eggs stuffed with glue.

Girls of the dirty morning, ticketed and spent,
you will be less at forty than at twenty.
Your living is a waste product of somebody's mill.
I would fix you like buds to a city where people work
to make and do things necessary and good.
Where work is real as bread and babies and trees in parks
and you would blossom slowly and ripen to sound fruit.

From BREAKING CAMP
Poems of the early and mid Sixties

A kid on her way

The kid wanders, dazzled by the crowd
that buzzes in the mirrored plushy hall,
matrons, rapists, cokeheads: winners all.
The rhythm of the games, now hushed, now loud,
is the catching and slow loosing of the breath.
The tables beckon, pools of sequined hands:
beautiful, your face of light commands.
Deaf to the scarecrow mutter of varied death,
sure her fist of baubles will reverse
the turning drift of hungers, she makes her play.
The croupier rakes her brilliant chips away.
She rises, dazed, to fumble her light purse.
Draw a face on the mirror. Look hard. Blink twice.
A bit more death won't kill you. Try the dice.

How you stare

Your smile is a rubber ball
bounding twice on each step.
Ah those little loves with zippers.
You stand dreaming,
a centipede on honey,
and lick one foot at a time.

Dismissal

For pissing on her sofa
and (one week later) spraying on her Danish rug
the lady has had her pumpkin cat
— a hairy please-eyed male marked with bars —
executed, by the appropriate organization.
This cat was beset by fleas
but cherished cheap red tuna and any lap.
His nose was an erogenous zone.
Last summer on the Cape he ran away
and her children yowled through the scrub pine.
He is better off this way, she says.
We all get rid of our retainers
when their love, or loves,
annoy us.

Lapsed

Never to close again
except between planes
when we match coins of lives.
Your eyes seamed with veins
are restless. Passengers
in a fast car
they flick flick.
My laugh jars
throat of dust
ripe puffballs
we used to step on
in pirates' woods.

Suppose I pounded the table:
your face is stamped on my sleep.
I grow out of you yet
a split tree that
underground drinks
the same black waters.
If you laughed?
If you yelled *Get your harpies
off my nape*?
If rising you opened your arms
like cupboard doors?
If you bit me?

Memory's a freakish bank
where embarrassing treasures
still draw interest,
gold and tinsel and radium.
Beneath the table circle
lost names crying
in permanent dusk.

Memory smells
like carefully dried love
where I shelter
inside failure's toughening husk,
where each one labors
secreting the amber
that turns gnats
and midges and stinging flies
into jewels.

Lipsky on Ninth Avenue

You look like a mad but polite Odessa angel
lost somewhere off the Cape of Random Fogs.
Perhaps a battleship sank you.
Perhaps you got tired.
Or a boy with a slingshot took you for a stork.
You had a message to deliver that you have forgotten:
prophecy? revelation? revolution? vision?
That is why you are hurrying.
That is why you walk so fast:
you used to have big grey wings like a sea gull.

The miracle

Your ghost last night
wiped from my sleep
as clean as chalk.
I woke. Moon ribbed the floor.
A hand wrote, Quit this mourning.
Driftwood of dreamspar
message torn from
the screams of gulls
told me you
had been born again.

A wasp stands in
heat soggy air
above beige grasses
dry as woodash.
I have lain here so long
my chest
is numb from earth.

Somewhere hair of gauze
eyes of a frightened jay
you are kicking
your shrill new hungers
and sucking watered milk.
Somewhere they are just starting
to tease your arms
with pins.

Clinic hallway

Six cubicles side by side.
In each the flat bed
of sheeted table,
chair, clothesrack,
receptacle for soiled gloves:
whorehouse parody.

Death is a present hum
like airconditioning.
A nurse pushes a cart
neatly loaded with
paper Dixie cups of faeces:
twenty-four diseases
going past my feet.
I am waiting
for the doctors
to assign mine.

Sunday evening

On Manhattan Bridge
soiled newspapers lift and close
like swimmers going down.
East River stinks.
My shut eyes see green suns
more potent than
that oily drop
sliding under the towers.
Traffic skirts
a rumpled car with a hole
where the driver's head arrived.
The air is scum
on the stone city.
Blood stalls
like the week end.
In Brooklyn
an old man (your father)
opens the cocks wide
on his dead wife's stove.

The simplification

A rolling tank of man, ramparts of flesh,
a capitalist, a federal reserve of food,
a consumptive disease fed with crane and bucket,
he trundled in a gnatswarm of obscene joke
with his wife slim and grave as a nursing doe
and children ripe at every stage in his globe of home.
Truly a happy fat man is loved and not envied.
Then his luck fell in. A mushroom minded doctor;
sweeping undertow; clash of warlord after
a game and a broken bottle uneyed his daughter.
His wife died slowest, an organ at a time.
He burrowed into work and having no god,
cursed no one. His labors flourished as the light
drained star by star from his world, and the cold settled:
complex useful works like steel limbs.
And he like an ancient wood trunk is becoming agate.
His face is burnished and dark, eclipsed sun
whose eerie silver mane of corona shimmers.
He is perhaps fatter. His cold touch burns,
and he is reluctant to touch and gentle with words.
Rooms revolve around him into silence.

August

How long can all
stand at impasse?
Not a ripple stirs the grass.
The bee in thick air stalls.
Breath clots my throat.
Not a seed drifts down or petal falls.
The sun embalms
in middle air a mote
static as a bubble trapped in glass.
Silence parches into thirst.
Out of these turgid calms
tornadoes burst.

August, submerging

Till that time when the late light burns the leaves
against the window where I eat alone
domestic comforts rub against my legs:
my desk, my work, my lamb chop and my silence
but then a current flows in through my hair.

Neon sparks kindle a spastic blaze
in streets that form swift canyons toward meeting.
The day's business runs off. Breasts and thighs
soak in the rising tide and eddy swollen.
Mirrors buoy from the dark my drowning face.

This is weather of sorry mating and sly attack.
The prize I'll haul from an aquarium of smoke,
shark or minnow, already bloats and stinks.
Up from the bottom tomorrow mauled and gashed
I'll come reeking, festooned with dying weed.

But the bracing set of current against my flanks
as filmy electric tentacles bush across:
now, only, I am graceful as falling water.
Season of dog and dogfish. Search no calendars.
I make the climate in which I freeze and burn.

Night of the bear and polar light

Into the wood black as a child's midnight waking
dropping bits of bread a step at a time.
Trees' grey ankles wade in the flooding moon,
quicksilver drips from cobwebs.
A shrike hammers its iron cry home in my nape.
The shadows knit. I can still go back.
Until in the shaggy cave of bark
the hide and slow heart of the bear's embrace.

The snowbirds sport with my bread in their honed beaks.
Mazes of wrought iron lace invent new paths.
The grass creaks with frost
frost at the marrow,
eyes grey and blinded with frost in the empty woods.
The smoky taste of honey coats my mouth.
I freeze here waiting for the bear's return.

Exactly how I pursue you

Turn once in this cave of prisms, turn.
Face me. Straw and broken glass like jam on your mouth.
The virginities of mirrors bleed you hollow.
Your spread hands strain the air.
You will not touch me.

Antlered dreams: hoofs drumming.
Moon glutted eyes grey as cataracts
wink from the webbed foot of the bed.
My hair is a net of hooks.
Reluctantly you sink in fearing quicksand.
Your eyes over mine won't shut:
mermaid in brown winds she floats and turns
dune hair and dappled shoulder: I can hold her too.
The gnarled ladder of my spine explodes in petals.
Pink nebulae swarm in my throat. The scent of grapes
although you cannot see me. My fingers
if you listen are white bees.
Sun melts on my tongue. I am shining and dumb.

Scrub pine, scoured air, flakemist on the mouth.
My footsteps are slowly eaten.
My breath whitens from stark boughs.
In the snow cave you crouch
weaving a net of hair to hold yourself
and dream of sugar skulls.

Running toward R

The night is funnel shaped
pouring narrow and swift before me for a mile.
My coat flaps with haste through squat January streets
where stalling cars groan and heave in the slush.
I enter your room already: spritz of hope.
The gates of your arms close on me.

The seconds knock on hollow wood in my throat,
morse of my steps explaining, urging.
I pound on your door: you are gone to someone else.
I meet myself returning. Ice water seeps drip, drip.
I knock again: you sit among ten ivory counselors
who pour into your ear ooze of caution, oil of my perfidies,
cram batting of present comfort. Wait!
I can confess with such nice arrangement
you'll cluck with pity to hear me.

Overhead I stream in a smoke colored wind,
Nike with sail wings blasting ahead.
Under I scurry with glass words scolding in my chest.
What enemy do I race white breathed
who blast my eyes with a blizzard of wish and gravel,
who have only myself to name as master fixer
That I love you and am too late to find it out.

EARLY, EARLY POEMS

I started writing poetry regularly and seriously when I was fifteen and my family moved into a larger house by far than we had ever lived in. For the first time, I had a room of my own with a door that closed and some measure of privacy. I was upstairs, with the roomers, while my parents were downstairs.

My earliest poems were rimed and romantic, mostly about dying. I graduated quickly to writing rimed and unrimed political poetry by the yard. I also wrote free verse about mystical experiences, although I had no label for them at the time, wrote about my family, my friends, Detroit, my fears and my problematic self. I have included a few poems from my senior year in high school. My poetry became more imagistic, more focused.

This section contains poems from high school, college and a couple of years after that. Some of the poems were part of my three Hopwood winning manuscripts at the University of Michigan.

Nocturne

A vase of peonies in a dark room:
I bury my face in their fragrance.
They are as cool as the underside
of a waterlily pad
that stares through jade smooth depths;
as cool as the touch of a marble ledge;
as the languid fringed ferns
that droop feathery tassels
in the basement of the forest;
as chill as the hand
the wandering moon lays on my arm at night.

They are as white
in the hot thick blackness of the room
as milk spilled in the shade;
as white as the mute swans
bowing over their reflections
while I watch from a cobblestone bridge
where the wind runs through my hair.

But in the center of each white fountain
stand a few crimson ears of petals
as if someone had laid a hand there
and bled a few bright drops,
as if someone had tried, for an instant
to cool the fever of pain
in the whiteness of the peony
stumbling to its moon
through a dark room.

Face in the mirror

Who am I? What am I? Tell me.
This pale dark rimmed face,
skim sallow, eyes underscored with purple bruises,
mouth too full, mouth too big
hair a black unruly ruff
I brush it slowly into a furry hood
holding the brush out after each stroke
to hear it retort wispily.
My eyes are darkly mournful,
an outside rim of black, then brown
around the black staring pupils.
My face is sick. I do not like it. It is not me.

Who am I? What am I? Tell me.
I have shed self after self
as a grasshopper swells
leaving dried brown leaves of bodies in the dust.
Inside each shield of self is the core,
alive, persistent, urged tropistically
toward light and warmth.
I lift myself like a blind worm
wondering which way next.

I have memorized many facts
but love none of them.
Forces stir in me.
I compress them until my brain boils.
I move uneasily in this thin awkward body
hitting against the back of my eyes
like moths against a lighted window.

Who am I? What am I? Tell me.

Committee hearings, 1952

Impassioned slogans shouted years ago
come bouncing back like balls hit off a wall.
I swear my oath on ill-deciphered scrawl
and hear fools take dead lines and rub and blow.

The committeemen sit growing, flicking ashes
while boredom spreads like oil. Only the clerks
are busy. The chairman makes a point and smirks
toward the camera saluting with their flashes.

He bangs his fist on wood demanding truth.
Admit! Recite! Renounce! Catharsis-wise
a string of balding men apologize
for the intellectual climate of their youth.

No lantern's light finds honesty in fear.
No phoenix is distilled from ashes here.

Lil's monody

It is never noisy on the eighteenth floor
but there is always sound
of typewriters tapping self-containedly
in blocks of offices, of voices through the doors
of inner offices, of whir of file drawers
opening and thudding when they shut.
the precise clatter of high heels across
a room and passing in the corridor.

In a morning not at all fresh and green
but like a conference room after a meeting,
thick with factory smoke rancid as cheap cigars,
I lay my purse — white for summer — down.
I sit at my little desk, the drawers
laid out with stacks of forms and vouchers,
pink for files, green for shipping,
yellow for service and white (like my purse
and shoes worn in the office) for the customer.

I stand at the sealed window envying pigeons.
I am a pupil in one glass eye.
Tarred roofs endure in all directions, multileveled
beneath a sky like a dirty plastic lid
where a naked bulb of sun sucks smoke.
A greening dome rises like a moldy breast
and hands of skyscrapers, stark
and smooth as headstones.
There juts an elbow of cramped holiness,
swarming with stunted saints and angels
and grimy broken gargoyles
Beyond it I can almost think I see
a blur of green that would be the cemetery.

It is to ground so shaken by traffic rumble,
to ground honeycombed by sewer and subway
I have resigned your body
to the gutted prostrate body of the city.

I walked among those graves last afternoon.
Among the slaughtered angels and anchored angles,
the titled crosses, urns, Corinthian pillars.
Down a gravel path I wandered,
stone gathering in my black shoes
Cicadas were shrilling from some shrunken elms.
Beyond the wrought iron fence
and the street where men are drilling for the expressway
that will sever this neighborhood limb from limb,
some was playing blues on an electric guitar
on the floor above the faith healer's sign.

Black solstice

The darkest god devours the bleeding sun.
Today ancestors leapt under an iron sky
through hilltop fires and the spring was won.
This sky seeps lower and my cinders die.

Wind scatters ashes on the rutted furrows
where shrunken seeds congeal into stone.
Moles and hares lie rigid in their burrows.
Death after death, I'm shriveling to a crone.

The shrunken heads of lovers, husbands, friends
hang like onions in the rafters. All my ends
have sputtered into silence. Though I burn
my house down, those I've lost do not return.

So late, so cold, the cost of light runs higher:
I strike a match and set my hair on fire.

October

The strong broad wind of autumn
brushes the leaves from the trees
fling them onto the carpet of lawns:
lawns littered with leaves like torn
paper bags, leaves like seared apple skins,
leaves like insect wings.

All across the hills
the hickories are hard yellow screams
shouting their incandescence.
The maples flame, the oaks ignite,
the elms drop scorched leaves.
Ivy dries and reddens on the wall.

There is lye in the wind
eating the flesh from the land
till the black skeletons arch against the grey sky,
till the earth's great backbone rears itself
picked clean of abundance, concealment.
Everywhere broken ribs of branches are strewn.
There is fire in the wind
turning all impurities to flame.

Storm outside, storm inside

What fury sweeps the scudding cloud
eastward over Whitefish Lake?
What swelling force sends arcs of blackbirds
wheeling over Whitman's Point
in swift and whiplike diagrams?

An anger folds the waves on wave,
their rounded humps smooth as enamel,
their teeth as white as crockery.
Whitman's point protrudes
and quits in a sullen pile of rocks
where waves slam and seethe and turn
and crash upon themselves again.

What fury shoves us brutally
toward each other? Only
this rage like fierce high wind
slamming the shutters, uprooting the shingles
flapping and ripping the canvas blinds.
Out in the torrent, a neighbor's dog
lifts his nuzzle to bay the wind,
wind that worries us, seeking
for the friction of body hard on body
as two stones cracking on each other
hit till one stone finds its flaw.

The ceremony

The sky is dark and the wind is rising.
The light, mottled black and yellow green,
oozes muddy glow through the tall windows.
Shall I draw the draperies, my lady?

There's a smoky rumble in the wind, audible
beyond our teacups faint decorous rattle.
The tea's a rich red-brown. Tapered ghosts
of steam drifts from each hollow pearl of cup,
your fingers, a Dresden curtsy on the handle.

Nevertheless, there's something in the wind
all our conversation laid our carefully
as silver for a dinner may not squelch.
The wind is impolite and mutters hungrily
dashing cinders hard against the panes.

Your pouring is a sacrament to pride
but the fire leaps and twists itself
and rises from its grate to hang in air.
If I could do it in the proper tone of voice,
I would point out the chandelier in the next
room has begun to swing in circles.

Lady, I am vexed by the temptation
to open the French doors wide and breathe
the acrid wind smoke down into my lungs.

Yet to sit here among a dozen rooms
reflected off the polished surfaces
of furniture and tea set, to sip tea
and to discuss the latest quarterlies
seeing your ring catch light, your eyes reply
is precious. Circe-like, you've strained reality
through your imagination and condensed
all objects to reflections on your eyes.
But how will you serve in the rubble, lady?
How will you make proper tea from ashes?

Don plays Mozart

He seizes the violin by its slender waist
and pushes it against his chin
with his large brusque hands
while the audience expects to see it
buckle like an accordion.
He scowls a command to his pianist.

Then his fingers are brown swallows
that swoop among the trees on a summer evening,
birds weaving swift and intricate loops of sound.

The music descends a white marble cascade
into a ballroom lit with fountains of candles.
It swirls in stately circles and pirouettes.
Lavender and musk are interwoven
in the strands of lacquered music.
Delicate moth feet tread decorous
elaborations among the dancers.
The music curtseys, dips, then lays a momentary
small white hand on your arm, drawing
your head down to hint
murmuring in the violin
that perhaps death is behind
that courtly enameled mask.
Under the elegantly curled and powdered wig,
perhaps it's death you're dancing with.

Then laughs, lightly, pianissimo,
flirts a brittle fan and taps a blue silk slipper
and whirls away dancing.
The tiers of candles flickers once, twice
polite and dim like a graceful gesture.

Then there is only Don
clutching the violin by its middle again
while his bespectacled accompanist
bows from the waist.

Woman with suitcase

If I stand upon a bridge
between the town and town
between the wet and dry stars
watching the moon down
although my mind dips like a branch
I do not plan to drown.

Through the waves I see a room —
luggage like my face —
but cannot think a fall would help
me jump to that embrace
or that once in that I should find
it ample enough space.

Walls of lights are galleries:
tableaux that simplify
or candles lit to mourn the lives
I touched but did not try,
frames of love and furniture
we shrink to occupy.

Yet were my elbows more boxed in
when I was locked and wed
than by the mazes of my need?
My hungers must be fed
whether I lie down tonight
in shared or rented bed.

Grand tour 1957

From Chicago through Ann Arbor to Detroit,
then east to New York I went by coach.
I retained a literary fondness for trains
far too long.

> At factories' blank and common backs I stare
> shocked to be uncertain if I'm there:
> each town looks like the last town
> from a night train eastward bound.
> Can't my blood cry to me from the ground?

I was making my own folk song,
all we sang then, from miners, sailors
sharecroppers, the Spanish civil war.
But I had grown up on urban blues
and Jewish liturgy. And turned away.

> Wind harvests what the prodigal sows
> if any of her salt seed grows.
> I burnt my flesh here and left no ash.
> I pass the graves of homes the crane has smashed
> to clean the way for glassy dominoes.

> In rotten blocks between the bridge's paws
> can any ghost of meaning walk these streets?
> Smogbleared foliage hanging in worn teats,
> spavined houses the traffic gnaws.
> The past tears in my hands like dirty gauze.

In Detroit public schools they told us
Antoine de la Mothe Cadillac founded
the city, but we knew it was Henry Ford.
I was going to Europe, where culture was stored in cathedrals
and made in cafes, where the Left was alive
I had read in a book by Sartre, consumed
illicitly in the philosophy department
hidden like a Batman comic
behind the text of Kant.
I wore black and lived on beans.

Pushing against the sun I rode east
retracing the steps of my grandparents
past slums where they were mocked, exploited,
fleeced, starved, beaten — and they survived.
They brought their culture with them in workers
circles, but me, I was a poet who knew
more French than Yiddish, more Eliot
and Whitman than Torah or Marx.

> When the spiked crown of New York sank in the sea
> grandparents davened and cursed in me
> wailing in my bones of treachery.
> Back to the butcherland which at such cost
> we fled. Now you go back. Our blood is lost.

> But American wrapped me up in cellophane.
> *I lug Detroit through France and Spain.*
> *My country distends and works in me*
> *inexorable as pregnancy,*
> *a heaviness that shadows all I see.*

> My voice clangs. *Moi, je suis americaine.*
> *A short lifetime of erosion brings me here.*
> *We used to scrape the good land bare and then*
> *move on to chase the blue frontier*
> *starting and starting and starting again.*

What I found among the cobblestones,
the bombed out streets, the ghettoes
squashed like egg cartons, the spires
and apses and domes, was myself:
a past that led bleeding toward me
a present in which I flourished in my poverty
like a flowering weed out of asphalt
and the word, the word, the future word
was being formed of my blood.
In me was the poet I will be.
In me were the words heating
hardening, the words
taking shape and growing
ticking in my womb
like a bomb.

UNCOLLECTED POEMS
Poems spanning several decades

The well preserved man

He was dug up from a bog
where the acid tanned him
like a good leather workboot.

He is complete, teeth, elbows,
toenails and stomach, penis,
the last meal he was fed.

Sacrificed to a god or goddess
for fertility, good weather,
an end to a plague, who knows?

Only he was fed and then killed,
as I began to realize as you
ordered the expensive wine,

urged lobster or steak, you
whose eyes always toted the bill,
I was to be terminated that night.

I could not eat my last meal.
I kept running to the ladies room.
All I could do was drink and try,

try not to weep at the table.
I was green as May leaves on the maple.
I was new as a never folded dollar,

a child who didn't know how the old
story always ended. Sacrificed
to a woman with more to offer up,

the new May queen, lady of prominent
family, like the bog man I was
strangled with little bruising.

I lay in my bed with my arms folded
believing my life had bled out.
How astonished I was to survive,

to find I was intact and hungry.
All that happened was I knew the story
now and I grew long nails and teeth.

Nightcrawler

Easy sleepers tucked in their white envelopes
with a seal that only dawn's alarm will break:
with envy I lift away the sides of houses.
Their snores arise like furry incense.

Shunted like a boxcar through broken switches
I rattle down prairie ghostlands of remember
past rusty flyblown sagging shingle towns
where the rusty sign of want creaks in the wind.

Floodlit by a blind eyeball of moon,
the past here is continuously performed,
an all night movie for insomniacs.
The floor is sticky with candy or with blood.

Voyeur, I spy on my own dead, performing.
Glued to that dim keyhole, I shout at them
Hold on! Put down that bottle. Toss those pills.
Next week a love letter will come with a check.

They don't listen. They break each other's
bones. They rub ground glass into their eyes
as blood flows out like satin under the door.
Always a phone rings in an empty house.

Easy sleepers, do ghosts ride your rails
all night telling stories you dread hearing?
This train runs backward toward old deaths
as fast as I pull forward toward new ones.

Red brick monument

All that's left is what we left,
house of red bricks narrow as a chimney
and crooked, leaning toward the East River.
Those dim steps creaked
as I went up heavy
as I came down giddy
as I went up burning
as I came down ashen.
Ajax Washing Machine Repair has moved away.
The view from the kitchen: rats' playpens.
Across the street wounded buses limp home.

Words, words fall on my face like soot.
We were comrades, we were friends, we were lovers.
We tied a strong rope of our lives
four strands transcending possession.
We ate crises like bagels for breakfast chewing and chewing,
a continuous meeting within a continual bust.
We washed our dishes in red suds.
We translated our purpose from each other
like braille newspapers in bed.

Only now the neighborhood begins to subside
from black ridges of powdered iron around a magnet.
When I pass nearby I think, they have renigged.
They have gone west with baggage of clinkers,
and I grin with emptiness.
The flesh and blood of that loving
was consumed in bitter electrical storm
but its shadow
like the imprint of a combusted body on pavement
has sunk into my bones.

Yet there is in the memory the crabbed beauty
of metal heated almost to boiling, then cooled.
In the ashes of a house, an old fashioned bathtub
waits like a boat
whose river has run dry
afloat on ashes instead.

Dream of order at the carnival

Each time at the top of the ferris
wheel we seem to hang a moment
among the stars dripping on our heads.

Below, in the rank alleys of concessions,
barkers' nasal come-ons, a woman shrieks,
cry soaring like a gull through neon foam.

Then we dip down, plunging, swinging
from our high perch into steamed
chaos, the smell of caramel corn

and hotdogs, manure and urine,
gunpowder as firecrackers go off
or is someone being shot?

Borne swiftly backward through the night
round and then up to bob again
like a tipsy minor moon, seeing

the ocean with the real moon sparking
a path on the waves to the world's edge,
the lights of a freighter on the rim.

Serenely we observe mayhem below
as if in five minutes we will not get off
among pink plush bears and local drunks,

as if from the top of this wheel of fortune
we could rise into the moon cool as angels
instead of being discharged at the base.

How easy is forgetfulness

Her flesh is snowing from her.
Light moist flakes small
as the points of straight pins
touch your skin fainter than any caress.

Icicle memories glitter and fall
smashing. Their weight
brings them down, and a change
of climate around her.

Her bones streak the night
like rising breath in the cold
as she evaporates
from your rooms and life.

Why do you gaze in the mirror,
look grave and then smirk?
Something us caught under your nails.
Then it is gone.

Eye contact

How your face cuts
my eyes. All else blurs
and your image burnt
into my retina like the sun
dances superimposed
on everything. When
your eyes brood on me,
I turn my face, I hide
in your shoulder.
Do I fear you will see
too clearly, too much?
Rarely have lovers
stunned me with insight.
The modeling of a cheek,
the strength of shoulders,
the gift of sensual ease
mean what they mean
like the scent of lilacs.
Yet my eyes ache
as if you stretched them.
Tears of release touch
them briefly as we lie still.
As I go from you down the
wrinkled street, I smile.

On technique

The poet has been lecturing
on the mysteries of the creative
process; the poet has been conducting
workshops, giving readings with light
streaming from the eyes and the gift
of fiery tongues descending. The poet
has been hammering out essays
on the fine critical oiled joints
of technique. Now like a woman
who danced wildly all evening at a party
wriggling her hips, bouncing her ass
around and comes home at last too tired
to fuck, she sits at her desk,
the sheet before her vast and white
in the avalanche of silence.
Then she figures out how to con
her muse and writes this poem
about the poet who has been lecturing
on the mysteries of the creative
process.

For a radical poet

Drops of water skitter
over an oiled surface and off:
words not coupling with the nerves, the muscle.
Irony is your tool, you explain,
inviting the unpersuaded into the poem,
a machine of irony which alters them.
How about you, hovering?
Politics in the belly changes
how we act with those
we have something to gain from or lose.

Alone you struggle with demons
discharged crackling from your brow.
What tax accountant of the blood
notes who supports your high privacy,
model, mother, servant, footstool, goat.

You want Blacks and Indians free
but your private life is private.
How you act with women is your own business.
Exactly. You own no stock in G.E.
You're no bank president battening on real estate.
But your larder is full of haunches that bleed.

That knot in the solar plexus,
that tight circuitry in the brain
of what feels natural
breeds poems like a nuclear reactor
breeds power, spewing hot waste
and a lasting taint
downstream.

I want you to understand why
I can no longer enjoy your poems
about revolution.

The music wars

Smog sweats from the streets.
The cacophony of sound boxes,
speakers in windows, car stereos
blasting, sticks up spiky
from among the people, metal
glinting, derricks madly pumping.

If we could shut off our ears,
turn down the volume control
on the night, what would we see?
A hundred thousand peacocks
each displaying his tail,
slowly turning, strutting, posing.

Hear my music: this is me:
this is my badge, my club,
these are my colors bleeding
on the air the way I mean it.
This is my identity I carry
like a banner through ash fields.

These are the words I would
shout at you if I could catch
them with my tongue; this
is the dance I would do
 before you all, my leap, my
riff, if my body knew how.

So each bird stands at the top
of his tree singing mine, mine,
signifying on the air to grab
some space that belongs to him.
We buy identity off the rack.
Everybody pays.

Between the end and the acceptance of the end

She has him like walking
pneumonia. How my bones ache
watching her in daily
labor to give birth to freedom,
unable to push hard enough.

You can stand at his shoulder.
See a man trying to get loose,
trying to scrape a woman off
like something he stepped in.
You can crouch behind her
as she kneels weeping. The lever
marked pleasure, the one she swore
allegiance to, now with perversity
she will not believe, shoots
into her spurts of electric pain.

A rat played the same tricks
learns, but the word love
fits over her head like a bag.
The children bang on her with fists,
punishing bad mommy who has begun
to weep and crawl, the wall
of the round world swung open
in a loud wind to let enter
the gunnery of the hail
the seige of the battering rain.

The air like stained glass cuts me

Lavender light laces through fretwork
of small panes, plucked boughs.
A burnt orange horizon is impaled
on Protestant steeples.
Bach suite for unaccompanied cello.
I am unaccompanied.
The scaffolding of the maple is striped bare.
The last leaves perch in the plane tree
huddling like robins that should have fled south.

I drink chardonnay from a glass
we bought together, wine
whose roots sprang from the soil
where you have set yourself like a sunflower.
The miles between us are doors
you have slammed, thousands of no's.

I wanted my love to warm you softly
as goosedown so your body could breathe.
I want my love to rest on you
lightly as falling maple leaves.
I want my love to show you your face
in a mirror of gold shining
from inside like the sun.

But you could not give credence to love
that did not seize you by your nape
shaking you like the assault of a tom cat.
You were suspicious of love that did not come
jangling labels like a janitor's keys.
You doubted a love open to the sky
as any planted fertile field.

The burning horizon slowly tamps out.
The snake's head of the needle strikes
blindly at record's end.
Where you walk it is afternoon still.
You cry *free* as the familiar walls drop in place.

In the cold sky Venus has just appeared.
Every evening my loneliness grows more porous.
Soon someone will slip through the fretwork
move in and start breaking the glasses you chose.
You could not love, but only redecorate.

Wise dreaming

Did you ever dream of someone
you have never met,
then meet that new penny face
on the first day of the new year?

I brought him home with me
that night, and still he stays.
His head rises with the morning
sun red through the pines.

There are times when our bones
know more than our brain,
when dreams rise up the spine
like the full moon sailing

its ivory balloon into velvet
darkness of the bedroom.
Sometimes we see clearly
what isn't, and then it is.

Man hung on himself

You stand like a black locust
graceful limbs of a dancer
but dead, bleak long after
other trees have leafed out.
I circle your tough supple
wood. Any day you must explode
into airy tracery of leaves,
long sweet panicles of blossom.
How you say, *come closer.*
Now you say, *keep away.*

I walk by your door
and someone is crying.
A jazz flute flirts
with its own embellishments.
A man bleeds words
through a great rent
in his side, that
he opens every night.
And now you say, *come in.*
And now you say, *stay out.*

You lie in my arms
and give me your lips
like a child, but you
clutch your rag of pain
tight like an old man
with nothing else left.
Your eyes are wide open
seeing nothing, no one.
And now you say, *love me.*
And now you say, *leave me alone.*

If this is a dance
you are both music
and dancer.
If this is a vision
it floats in your mirror.
Truly you must open
your own doors and windows
or lock them tighter.
And now you say, *touch me.*
And now, *I am always alone.*

I vow to sleep through it

I hate New Year's Eve.
I remember the panic to have
something, anything to do,
some kind of date
animal, vegetable, mineral,
a giant walking carrot,
a boa constrictor, a ferret,
an orangatang, a lump of coal.

I remember ringing apartment
bells on 114th Street
looking for a rumored party.
Parties with lab punch:
mogen david, grapefruit juice
and lab alcohol, hangovers
guaranteed to anyone within
ten yards of the foaming punchbowl.

I wake the next morning
with my mouth full of mouse
turds and wood ashes.
I wake and remember
how I tried to demonstrate
the hula, my hips banging
like a misloaded washer,
how I necked with a toad.

I remember limp parties,
parties askew, everyone
straggling home with the wrong
mate, the false match.
Evenings endless and boring
as a bowling tournament
at the senior center.
Is it midnight yet?

Only nine thirty? Only
nine thirty-eight? At midnight
we will spill drinks on
each other's clothes, kiss
the boors and bores we detest,
the new year like a white
tablecloth on which a drink
has already been spilled.

Midsummer night's stroll

The attenuated silvery evenings of northern summer,
they are at once languid and fierce, white Persian
cats preparing to mate. They are pale lilies
whose fragrance paints the air of a bedroom.

The light is milky, suave and must be entered.
Who can sit inside with the lights on?
This mauve sky wants to soak through your skin.
Your body will float like a cherry blossom fallen

on a slowly moving mirroring river.
This glow will not tan but lighten your flesh
till you find yourself borne up as pollen.
Words escape you like birds startled awake.

Your lover's face floats on this dusk, an alien
moon. You rise and vanish in the sky like a balloon.

Diptych

1. Reflections on a mirror

Mirror mirror on the wall
Bathroom mirror in which I sought
to catch my own nakedness
at twelve as black hair
began to tangle like briars
over the triangle where my thighs
met, mirror where my early breasts
gleamed absurd as lemons.

Mirror in which I would glimpse
sometimes another world under
lying this one, a shadow
world of grey women peering
over my shoulder, a world
where light broke in waves
on the window of morning
where night's chocolate melted.

Mirror to which I said NO
I will not be sucked thin by you
like a sour candy. I will
not fall into your dim waters
and drown in my own eyes,
I will not seek my smirk
in you as I pass through
restaurants, parties, halls.

Mirror where I stood with candles
burning on either side and promised
myself I would dive through
appearances into the dark waters
lapping beneath you, all the way
down into the octopus cave
where I would seize my own self
like a precious living conch.

Now I have aged in you
like something softening under
water, a gradual blurring
of lines and boundaries.
You have little left to give me
yet I love how you capture light
and fling it back. In you
the world turns half around.

2. Turn about

In the twilight of the room
the mirror beckons like a pond.
Dive in. Pass through.

In that room on the dark
side of the mirror moon
are all the things you lost.

Piles of keys on and off
their chains. Gloves.
Mufflers, umbrellas, hats.

Books and notebooks
full of words you could
never again conjure up.

Friends who will never
betray you in this wan
half faded world turned

about on its axis.
Love that wore out
like shoes in which

you walked much too far.
Promises now finally
redeemable like coupons.

If only you can remember
how to pass through the glass
like gauze curtains that tear

before you, like water
parting to let your warm body
drown in its cool embrace.

The diminishing addition

It's a madness that comes over us every seven
years, whenever we might lay some money by.
Instead we are contemplating our cramped kitchen,
frowning at the dark stuffy scruffy bedroom
and the urge strikes: imagine a bay window,
a sunroom, a deck, a bathroom: an extension.

The key work is tension. The desire
to screw up one's life, to rip a large
hole in the walls and let chaos in;
to riddle the fabric of existence with the chug
of cement mixers and the banging of hammers,
the roar of ghetto blasters tuned

to stations you hate. Oh, why can't we
resist? Shoot it up the nose, stick it
in our arm, drink it by the gallon
throw a large party and invite the marines
and the local high school, just start
a fire and barbecue a rat over the coals

of banked up dollars. But no, the fantasies
of more living room drive us as mad
as Hitler, only we are weak foolish Poland
invaded by mechanized armies of builders
wielding power tools, defended by cavalry
of our outraged cats. More couples break up

while renovating than at any other time,
a carpenter tells me, grinning. An addition
is first a subtraction, then a widening
division with floors that tilt like a ski slope,
ceilings that leak like the economy.
Carpenters who say they will finish tomorrow

then take a Caribbean cruise, with plumbers
harder to capture than Bigfoot, plasterers always
coming and never arriving, electricians
whose bills would bankrupt the Pentagon,
mortgage bankers, building and health inspectors:
all the invaders who make my home a house.

I have offended

Mocking my quibbles with beetle
flights of laugher, you have slammed
and flung open the doors of my mind
these five nights, mother of wolves
and words, kicking my ribs as I dozed.

You gave into my hands something
I scrupled to take. I swaggered
to find some lust I'd blink at,
polishing my weird little virtue
like a glass eye. Now in my palm

it is yellow as a wasp and stings,
respectability's prosthesis, blind
but keeping up appearances. Abstinence
is stuck uneasily on my peasant head
like a mortarboard on a pumpkin.

My own virtues are gamy fierce coyotes
who slink now cunning with want.
Shortly they will run amok in the sheep,
gone wrong through an overdose of caution
and bourgeois morals, like poisoned bait.

In long drought

With a scorched groan
the pump just failed.
For seven weeks no rain has fallen.

The sun cracks stones.
Dust blurs the sky,
clouds the leaves' clear green.

The beans form shriveled.
The shoots of the onion lie down.
The corn sags with frizzled hair.

The house is a series of thirsty vessels: the sink, toilet, tub
                     plants hose, kettles,
                     pitchers, pans, vases
                     glasses, buckets, the cats
                     and me.

My skin flakes into ants.
The bed is wrinkled as parched corn.
The kitchen smells like a compost pile.

I dream of water
seeping through the withered reeds of my muscles.
I imagine water
arching pell-mell down the waterfall of spine
water
percolating through the marshy net of my capillaries
water
roaring white as it rolls over and kicks up in foam
with a clatter of pebbles and spume dashed in my face.
I hear water
dropping like chimes from every leap of the maple
trickling among mossy stones where tall bugs skate
I see water

riding the wind in long skeins of pale wool
hanging sheets in midair, plastering my shirt to my ribs.
I feel water
washing over my parched and sandy skin
soaking into the cracked adobe of my mind.

Loosen the rain on us!
The sun has become a grimace. An absence
stronger than any presence
is long drought.

The correct method of worshipping cats

For her name is, She who must be petted.
For her name is, She who eats from the flowered plate.
For her name is, She who wants the door always opened.
For her name is, She who must sleep between your legs.

And he is called, He who must be played with until he drops.
He is called, He who can wail loudest of all.
He is called, He who eats also from your plate.
He is called, He who sleeps in the softest chair.

And they are known as eaters and rollers in catnip
Famous among the nations for resonant purring.
Feared among the mouse multitudes. The voles
and moles also do run from their shadow.

For they perform cossack dances at four a.m.
For they stick their faces in your face and meow.
For they sit on the computer monitor to monitor your work.
For they make you laugh with their silly acrobatics
but their dignity is that of the oldest gods.
Because of all this we are permitted to serve them.
We are the cat servants, some well trained and some ill,
and they give us nothing but love and trouble.

The name of that country is lonesome

We go to meet our favorite programs
the way we might have met a lover,
the mixture of the familiar routine
and the unexpected revelation.

We can buy love at the shelter
if we get there before they have
executed it for being unwanted,
its fur cooling in the garbage.

It becomes more and more unusual
to be invited to dinner;
fast food is the family feast.
Who can be bothered with friends?

They have needs, you have to remember
their birthdays, they want to talk
when you're just too tired.
Leave the answering machine on.

No one comes to the door any longer.
We would be scared.
That's why we have an alarm.
That's why we keep the gun loaded.

Drive in food, drive in teller,
drive by shooting, stay in the car.
Talk only to the television set.
It tells you just what to buy

so you won't feel lonely
any longer, so you won't feel
inadequate, bored, so you can
almost imagine yourself alive.

Thou shalt not complain
about anything I might have to fix

It's always embarrassing when some woman
rolls up her blouse sleeve to show you a bruise
not sexy even, just colored like a charcoal
sunset, the fingerprints of pain.

We have been trained to ignore the cries
through the motel wall. After all, maybe
he's paying for it. Some women like
to be hurt. You know how cats sound then.

It is as if she stripped in the committee room,
so awkward, so tiresome, her trouble
scattered around the room like used
underwear, not bustiers but nylon slips.

It's comfortable here in my office,
the corner office finally. It's cosy
on my twenty-fourth floor with balcony,
here in the compound with a guard at the gate.

You weep into my telephone, leaving
desperate messages on my answering machine.
You write me long handwritten notes
I throw into the paper shredder.

You buttonhole me in the hallway,
stand beside my table while I consume
my brioche, march outside with signs.
I step into your hard luck on the street.

Don't you understand your pain bores
me? I am all for free expression
except for those who whine,
who weep, who moan, who scream.

I will listen gladly to any complaint
I share; I will sign on for any charity
I don't have to smell. I only object
to demanding change from me.

Always unsuitable

She wore little teeth of pearls around her neck.
They were grinning politely and evenly at me.
Unsuitable they smirked. It is true

I look a stuffed turkey in a suit. Breasts
too big for the silhouette. She knew
at once that we had sex, lots of it

as if I had strolled into her diningroom
in a dirty negligee smelling gamy
smelling fishy and sporting a strawberry

on my neck. I could never charm
the mothers, although the fathers ogled
me. I was exactly what mothers had warned

their sons against. I was quicksand
I was trouble in the afternoon. I was
the alley cat you don't bring home.

I was the dirty book you don't leave out
for your mother to see. I was the center-
fold you masturbate with then discard.

Where I came from, the nights I had wandered
and survived, scared them, and where
I would go they never imagined.

Ah, what you wanted for your sons
were little ladies hatched from the eggs
of pearls like pink and silver lizards

cool, well behaved and impervious
to desire and weather alike. Mostly
that's who they married and left.

Oh, mamas, I would have been your friend.
I would have cooked for you and held you.
I might have rattled the windows

of your sorry marriages, but I would
have loved you better than you know
how to love yourselves, bitter sisters.